DON'T BLAME ME!

by

PETER BLYTH

Moyhill Publishing

© Copyright 2019 Peter Blyth

All rights reserved. No part of this publication may be reproduced, stored in a retrieval system, or transmitted, in any form or by any means, electronic, mechanical, photocopying, recording, or otherwise, without the written prior permission of the author.

First Published in 2008 by *Moyhill* Publishing
A CIP catalogue record for this book is available from the British Library.

Printing History
First Published in 2008
Electronic Book Edition 2019

Designed & typeset by *Moyhill* Publishing

Acknowledgements

Thank you to the following who have helped me to make this book possible:

Bryan McHugh (now in spirit), who kick-started me on my journey; Ralph Mckintyre, a good friend and an excellent counsellor (Shoreham UK); Carol McHugh; Violet King, for giving me inspiration from her book *Change Your Life... do it today!;* and to Duncan Page and family, for his constant unconditional love and support.

My family, past and present; especially to my brother Stephen and little Frejya for smiling and keeping us happy; not forgetting Aunty Rachel (for her inspiration); and my parents (in spirit), who started this grand fiasco!

Sir Norman Wisdom, Ken Dodd and all my theatre friends, for a good laugh!

Hollywood life-coach Michael Neill (his book *You can have what you want*), for his beautiful smile and genuineness; and to Paul McKenna and Dr Richard Bandler for their hypnotic thoughts.

Sgt Peter Darkin and PC Paul Taylor for their past support in a difficult occupation.

All the rest of my family and friends, too many to mention without a separate book!

But most of all, thank you to *ME* for being *ME*... at last!

Peter Blyth
Internationally Fully Licensed NLP practitioner. ADV cns (M.A.S.C.) Psycology and stress management. OU.

Love and light to all.

Contents

	Introduction	*1*
1.	Get out of that rut!	3
2.	The blame game	7
3.	But. but. but. but. but…	11
4.	Drowning your sorrows in the swim!	15
5.	Just stop!	17
6.	No pain	21
7.	Burn the witch within	25
8.	Twiddling your thumbs!	29
9.	Two Policemen and a Norman Wisdom song!	33
10.	Accept. Accept. Accept.	35
11.	Just get out there and live a little	39
12.	Designer labels	43
13.	Bloody 'ell, it works!	47
14.	Meditate to mediate	49
15.	The grand finale	53
	The author	*55*
	Useful Websites	*57*

Introduction

Don't blame *ME*...

How many times have we said or heard that? Many I am sure, but you know it's actually a very powerful statement to blurt out when we feel our hackles going up, or feel that we are being pushed into a corner when someone else starts to play *THE BLAME GAME* (see Chapter 2)

This book has been written in the style of a work book, with various NLP and other exercises, so that you can explore your own *BAGGAGE* and get rid of it... once and for all!

We have all been on our roller coaster journeys in life and sometimes we need to...

...JUST STOP...

...for a while, and reflect what's going on in there – in our heads – and then look at how we can change it for the better.

So! Sit back and enjoy the ride of your life... and go with the flow to change your inner and outer selves forever...

Good luck!
Peter.

Chapter 1

Get out of that rut!

Are you positive or negative today?
Have you ever really thought about this? Are you going around in a negative guise (*IN A RUT*) or are you being *positive* in your thought processes.

The unconscious mind has a habit-forming department, and if you go about your daily life thinking *negative* things – whatever they might be – your mind will quickly adapt and apply this attitude to *everything you do*.

You may have seen Noel Edmonds on TV recently – since he re-surfaced with "Deal or no Deal" – in this, he does a thing called *cosmic ordering*. Well, this is a form of positive thinking. When he gives out a *positive* thought, it creates energy and this is *Positive* energy, which has a knock-on effect on the rest of the day's events.

So. What sort of person are *you*? A frequently asked question – but the *real* question should be "*what sort of person have YOU ALLOWED YOURSELF TO*

BE". Personal responsibility comes in here; otherwise we will spend our lives *BLAMING* others.

Just for as moment, try re-programming (NLP) your mind to think positively:

Exercise
Take a piece of paper with you when you go about your day.

Divide the paper in two columns and every time you think *down* of yourself, or others, – or about an event you are about to do – make a note, in the left hand column, of how you felt it went. Remember to give the event a title; e.g. a meeting with someone; a decision to buy or not to buy; how you felt when you got out of bed and planned (or not) your day;... and make a note of that too.

Note everything you can on this one day.

Then tomorrow...
Check your notes and everywhere you see a *NEGATIVE* write opposite it at least five other ways *you* could have done it differently... *DON'T BLAME ANYONE!*

Just compare the *ALTERNATIVES*.

Then, if possible, re-do the event or action in the *NEW LIGHT*.

Good Luck...

How do *you* see the world.....?

An optimist sees a glass as half full
A pessimist... as half empty
How do *you* see it?

Optimist
I see the world as being full of vibrant energies and colours.

Although bad things may happen, we all learn by them, making us a better people from the knowledge of that particular event.

We can build mountains out of mole-hills if we take positive steps forward, rather than negative ones backwards.

Learn lessons from the past; move on and forget it; remember that every living thing in this universe has been sent by great spirit to enhance our lives, and maybe we need the sadness, together with the happiness, in order to progress to the equilibrium of the spirit world.

Pessimist
This world is getting worse. It seems full of war and killings, and full of ignorant people who never help anyone, we all must be selfish these days to survive.

I've just missed my bus, they are always late.

It's raining and wet, I feel miserable, and no one ever talks to me, and when they do they always moan and groan. I *hate* that, why can't people be happy...

They never are!

Which way of thinking do *you* prefer?

A message to the pessimist!
Missing the bus may give you an opportunity to talk to people who are also in the queue, thus maybe helping you to make new acquaintances...

Rain helps the plants grow making it a healthier and more beautiful place to live:

Listen to the birds singing – when it has been raining – and look at the colours of every rainbow.

Chapter 2

The blame game

SO! Let's play The *BLAME GAME*...
Its simple. You need at least one player...

YOU!

And / or another...
...or better still, a whole family...

Lets begin
Go about your daily life spitting venom, moaning and groaning about how it was his or her fault.

WHY... the great accusation word
Why didn't *they* do this, or why didn't *they* do that, if *they* had done this or that, things would, should (oops the should is shit word again) have been different...

We all do this, and some of us do it for most of our lives.

All that this *Blame Game* does is to create *negative* emotional turmoil in our heads, causing those famous little voices to enter our souls (actually our egos) and *BLAME BLAME BLAME!*

Well. Guess what? There's a simple way to *STOP* this happening...

Reframe the Blame
First, gauge the blame:
Score from 0 (none) to 10 (a lot of blame!)
Number..........?

Sit quietly and – either with a trusted friend or just you – close your eyes. Place the thoughts of blame into a picture frame in front of you – make a list beforehand if you like – then see if those memories are in *colour, black & white, moving* or *still*.

What sort of image feeling do you get?

Then...
Place this frame inside a *thick black* frame and move it to one side of your mind, in front of you... *TAKE OUT ALL THE SOUND & COLOUR AND DISTORT THE PICTURE AS MUCH AS YOU CAN.*

Then...
Picture a really *good* event that brought you intense pleasure (good sex is a good one, if you remember that!), or any *good* event that brought you lots of laughter and fun times. Give these pictures lots of colour, laughter and sound – happy voices and visions.

Build this up and up, *stronger* and **stronger** *brighter* and **brighter**.........

Then...
Push the negative blame picture in its entirety out in front of you, so it gets smaller and smaller, weaker and weaker... out to the horizon... out to sea, if you like.

Then...
Get the *good, BIG,* happy picture, place it in a catapult... pull it back... stretch it back... ready to fire it into the negative picture destroying it for ever...

READY...!
FIRE...!
BBBZZZZZZZZZZZZ BANG...
(Make this sound loudly as you do it)

Open your eyes quickly and gauge the thoughts now... Have they gone or reduced?

Repeat this until they are at 0!

Good Luck

The self

    The need to know the self
    The need to find the self
    The need to be the self

Be yourself
    The need to ask the self
    The need to tell the self
    The need to see the self

Be yourself
    The need to thank the self
    The need to sell the self
    The need to buy into the self

Be yourself
    The need to start the self
    The need to stop the self
    The need to prompt the self

Be yourself
    The need to create the self
    The need to ornate the self
    The need to stimulate the self

Be yourself
    If you can see yourself
    And you can judge yourself
    And you can accept yourself
    Then you *are* yourself.

Chapter 3

But. but. but. but. but…

…that internal motor bike!!!!

Go on. Try and say *but* over and over again, very quickly… Are you a Yamaha or a Honda? You sound just like an internal motor bike. Don't you?

"What's one of them?" I hear you say.

Well, an internal motor bike is a group of thoughts – *negative* ones of course – like the *WHAT IF's*.

They come into our heads when we have *self doubt*; when we go around in our lives, in a negative frame of mind, thinking that we can't do it because of this or that reason. Isn't it about time you decided that in actual fact – as my dear mum used to say…

> *THERE'S NO SUCH*
> *THING AS CAN'T?*

To remind us of this situation, we often see, on television, people with incredible disabilities who climb mountains, drive cars without a lower half to their body... yes it IS true; there is a woman in America whom I would love to meet, who was born without a lower half to her body – nothing from the waist downwards. Incredibly, this woman gets around her town on a skateboard, and drives on the roads in America (rather her than me) in a big truck, and has no problem with feeling happy and confident.

How do you *do* that?

The answer is within you. You need to constantly remind yourself how lucky *YOU* are...

Go on, close your eyes and say to yourself...

HOW LUCKY I AM...

...and then repeat it ten or more times.

If you have any "doubting Thomas" voice that comes in to argue, write down what it says and then place it next to a person in a worse situation than yourself. Bet your bottom dollar that when you do this, such a person or event will come on to the TV – or you will go down the street an see such a thing or person – worse off than yourself.

Go on. Try it NOW!

Well? Did you see them? What does that tell you?

Sometimes you have to take a risk to get there! allbeit a calculated one. If you don't try, you will never find out.

But. but. but. but. but…

Remember

There's no such thing as failure! That word belongs on *"the Blame Game"* page!

Okay, it didn't work? So lets try it this way –

Be POSITIVE

GO FORWARD

*AND TRY IT **again…***

and again… and again!

Every time you say the BUT word, fine yourself a pound – or a Euro.

You will become a positive thinker or a millionaire! Either way, it worked! Didn't it?

Don't blame me!

So what are you really searching for?

What are you really searching for?
What do you wish to gain?
If you sit back and look again
You will find it without pain…

What are you really searching for?
Do you really want to know?
Or is it better to take your time?
And just go with the flow…

For years we have been guiding you
Through all your pain and wails
To have a more relaxing time
And move more like a snail…

Just stop and think and watch and learn
A listening ear is good
For your own good health and welfare
Just slow down, as you should

You see the others rushing too and fro
They haven't gained the art just yet
Of taking things more slow…

So patience is the learning curve
For you to see this day
And stop that silly searching
And just relax and play

A poem received from spirit to myself in 1995.

Chapter 4

Drowning your sorrows in the swim!

You know that every time we have a *bad* event in our lives we tend to remember it in detail. We bury it into our good old sub-conscious mind, only for it to be resurrected at a later date.

Well, of course, when we have a happy event we also tend to bury that – in our *good* memory bank– and also forget it.

We can, and do, of course, resurrect the good times consciously, to tell others about it. *BUT* do we do this with the bad events? *A BIG NO* comes across your brow I see!

Hiding the unconscious thoughts of negativity is done by our brain very easily and it is only when we feel down, or depressed, that they surface again, only this time in a different form – i.e. different chemicals in the brain give off a different image or feeling

Don't blame me!

The other day, the local swimming pool re-opened for the winter season and I suddenly realised how *de*-stressing – and not *dis*-stressing – swimming actually is. Having recent events surface as we humans do, I decided to conduct an experiment.

Whilst swimming up the pool, I thought of the bad or negative event and as I breathed and swam. By just thinking of it… guess what? It got worse, building up an even bigger resentment of the person I was actually thinking about.

I then swam back to the other end, this time, as I did so, I breathed in with the word "*PEACE*" and out with the phrase "*let it go*" and guess what? This time the resentment *DID GO*!

This system can work for any problem, or group of problems, in your life. As you swim, the chemicals and emotions are aroused and as such – with the increase in heart rate and body fluid (blood etc.) circulation, – are changed, thus relaxing the thought and emotion process.

So, *GET* that old cossi on and take yourself off to the baths and have a good *LETTING GO* session in the pool. Drown your sorrows with swimming, rather than other systems such as booze.

Chapter 5

Just Stop!

Do you ever get so wound up in your day that you find your concentration going banana's – or your emotions ready to boil over – causing anger, frustration and a total lack of self-esteem and control?

What do you mean, *"every"* day!

Well, there is a simple answer to this one – and *DON'T* tell me *"OH I NEVER HAVE TIME"* ... cos *YOU DO!*

STOP! STOP! STOP!

Whatever you are doing... Unless saving a life... or delivering a baby... *Stop!* Sit down and meditate for as long as you can – even five minutes a day is enough to prevent serious illness, or even *death by stress*! Far worse than *death by chocolate,* I can assure you.

Sit down, put some music on if possible – any will

do – you don't have to buy expensive meditation discs, just music that you enjoy, or even a good book.

Shut off the phone, switch off the doorbell and, above all, switch off the mobile! (Blasted things…)

Then, allow yourself to float away into dreamland and see what visualisations you can do.

Be in a country lane or at the beach or anywhere you remember to be a peaceful relaxing place of your delight.

YOU MUST totally stop – and then ask your mind just to   s l o w   d o w n ,   and stop.

Slower and slower, until you have emptied the entire buzz from your head.

Don't worry, if this doesn't happen the first time. You really *will* see some results and with *DAILY* practice, you will be amazed how quickly you can reach the *ALPHA* state of sleep, commonly known as meditation.

We are all busy, in some way or another, but *WE ALL* have space for our own *right* to a quality of life, regardless of what the bully boss thinks, or the controlling colleague says, or indeed the doubting Thomas…

Take some quality time out for YOU!

Just Stop!

You get one hit at life, so enjoy the ride – it's over all too quickly otherwise.

Stress can be formed in various ways, but imagine this: A ladder; the bottom rung is peace and tranquillity; the top rung is the highest level of stress, and a heart attack and death…

As we climb our daily ladder, we must consciously take a downward step, back to ground level, otherwise – if we keep rising – we will reach heaven and meet God!

I am convinced that many employers want us to keep climbing the ladder in order that they will only have to pay out 50p for our funeral flowers rather than a lot more for our ongoing pensions… Which do *you* prefer?

SO STOP, RIGHT NOW,

…and descend that ladder in your daily meditation.

I've died and gone to heaven!

I've died and gone to heaven
Its very nice you know
To look down at you all on earth
And see you move so slow…

Up here we move so quickly
From place to place and more
We see it all in one big glow
That would make your brains quite sore…

If you could only now be with us
We could teach you all so much
In seconds… several lifetimes
Within your hearts you'd touch…

The energy is amazing
It is so bright and warm
Your healing power down there on earth
Makes us feel so… Forlorn…

So when you fear of dying
Please make sure that you know
When you pass on into heaven
Its very nice you know...

Received from spirit to myself in 1995.

Chapter 6

No pain

Whilst training for my NLP practitioner course with Michael Neill and Dr Richard Bandler, and... oh yes, of course, Paul McKenna – (look into my eyes..., you know the one) – one of the things that was constantly made clear was... why go through the pain during counselling and therapy, when you don't have to put things right?

I can hear all you freudalists say *"you must look at issues internally to rid yourself of the pain..."* Sorry, but what poppycock! We have, or at least *I* have, moved on from those dark ages of electric shock treatment for being gay or for phobia's and obsessions...! Haven't YOU?

Why on earth do you want to experience *more* pain from the original incident, or thought, when you can *just reframe it or squash it*... NLP... some call it life coaching.

We in the trade are nearly all *injured healers*. In other words, we have been though that old pain barrier and come through the other side. So, when you want to change the way you *FEEL* you do *not* need to look back into it, *just change it* for a better feeling. Use the *"reframe"* or *"squash"* exercise to do this for anything.

Some of you may be saying *"I tried that but it keeps coming back..."* Well, *keep trying* and you, as a UNIQUE individual, will find the method that works for *YOU*, as we are all very different.

NLP tells us that *"The Map is Not The Territory"*, which means that, we may all walk down a street, in London, say, but we will all see the things in that street in a very different way. With *pain* we have all gained that split-second memory of an event in a different way. So we can use our senses to describe it and then use our *subconscious* to find a solution to ELIMINATE THE PAIN, PERMANENTLY, from deep *inside the subconscious mind*.

If (in your view) the pain has been caused by another person then, rather than *blame* them – and carry the resentment on... and on and on... – place them in a *Happy Box* and reframe them... *HOW?*

The Happy Box...
Gauge the not-happy person from 1 to 10 as usual:

Close your eyes and imagine three boxes, or area's, one with friends you *really like* a lot; one with friends

No pain

you are *sort-of* okay with; and the other with the person mentioned above.

Now, move the person who you are *not* happy with OUT of the *not-happy* box and INTO the *sort-of-happy* box. Then move all of the people *including* the *not-happy* friend INTO the *Happy Box*.

BBBBZZZZZZZZ ... BANG!

Open your eyes and gauge the not-happy person again. Has the resentment gone with the pain? Keep going until it's at 0...

Good Luck!

Remember
It serves *no* purpose at all to carry pain, or to re-enter it...

*JUST DROP IT...
AND CHANGE IT TODAY, FOREVER!*

Chapter 7

Burn the witch within

Cherish the thought, well really! Sorry white witches... don't mean you.

What I am really talking about here is getting rid of those burning resentments that we all carry around with us from time to time... no no no matron, not all the time!

In our heads we have a little box for storing things such as resentments, this is a cousin to Mr and Mrs BLAME... and there's only one way to get rid of them: BURN THE BLINKIN THINGS!

So, off you go now and make a list on paper of all the resentments you can think of. Remember, its your own private list so you can put anything – or more importantly *ANYONE* – on it! (Don't forget to gauge them from 1 to 10.)

Stretch yourself here and really make a very *long* list, at least 30 – yes 30 – and then go into a safe place, outside. Get a lighter and set fire to the list… and as it automatically leaves your hand – instead of burning your fingers – SHOUT, AS LOUD AS YOU CAN…

> *I let go, PERMANENTLY
> of these, and all other
> "F……" resentments.*

Yes I do mean the F word… the more that it shocks you to use the "F" the better. If you are hung up about that then this is another resentment from the past and you can burn it with the rest… It's only a word!

NOW re-gauge… is it at 0…? If not, do it again, and again, until your witches have all flown off on their ignitable broomsticks and burnt!

Remember

Carrying resentments around with us daily and hourly only *CAUSES* us pain, as the resentment itself (person, happening, event, etc.) is *ALWAYS* unaware of being one!

> *Resentments are bad,
> Resentments are pain,
> So, if they return
> Just burn them again!*

P.S. All of these things change the chemicals (thoughts) in our brain for the good. We are made of one big chemistry shop and thoughts and emotions are formed by mixing chemicals in our brains. What NLP does is change the chemicals from bad ones to good ones... *permanently*.

Don't blame me!

Here is a reading I received from spirit, which refers to my astral flying as a child. Many of us have experienced this but only in later years do we recognize it. Try a thought before you go to sleep and see if you can fly.

Flying...

When I was young I used to fly
Down the stairs up to the sky
Through the clouds and over the fields
Looking down at all earth's yields

When I was young I used to dream
Of how the future world would seem
Who would I be what would I do
Where would I go would I meet you

So off I go upon my flight
To try and get all things right
But its not easy to make things flow
As there are always things which you don't know

As we pass through those early years
We all will shed so many tears
Some happy but some oh... so sad
We move on through our lessons glad

So we have all met challenges great
That help our journey incarnate
For when we move to other planes
We all can show how much we've gained

To those who meet us as old friends
And show us that there are no ends...

Chapter 8

Twiddling your thumbs!

Do you ever get bored at home, or wherever you are at the time? Well I do and a way to think about this, is simply to accept that what *is* simply *is*.

By this I mean that we create our own atmosphere or surroundings – don't we? Or do you believe that all our world has been decided for us by the great creator? Whatever the situation, what *is* just *is* and the only ones that can change this are ourselves.

When you sit at home, do you start to go in downward spirals of felling sorry for yourself, into that good old *RUT* again? Well, as the old song goes…

Pick yourself up,
Shake yourself down,
And start all over again.

…because the last minute of your thoughts has now *gone* and will never return, except in memory recall – which is debatable as to its importance.

Get out of that chair *NOW*, and instead of contemplating whether or not to drive to "so and so", or if to go to "whatchamacallit"...

JUST DO IT!
Go on, take that risk again and...DO IT!

Turning the *negative* thought process into the *positive* one really *is* that simple. As the tranquil sage stated... *Don't dwell on the past, or yearn after the future, for to live in the present time is... auspicious.*

There's a whole big world out there you know so whilst you are able, as you never know what's around the corner...

GET OUT   GET OUT   GET OUT
and
ENJOY   ENJOY   ENJOY
Today!
Right Now!

Go out and engage in conversation with someone new to you – see how interested you become in what they have to say – and *listen,* and maybe learn from them. If you find yourself going into the *me me's,* then your ego has taken control and you need to *STOP* again. Refocus and *listen* to them, however boring it may become. Train your brain to *listen* rather than show off *you*! This is a very good exercise for both the soul and the ego

Another good tip is when you learn something new or get a good positive thought or idea – as Michael Neill says –

> **WRITE IT DOWN**
> **WRITE IT DOWN**
> **WRITE IT DOWN**

If you are following the gist of my tips as you read through this book, you will by now be feeling much *More Positive... and happier...*

> *There's no sense in worrying*
> *Or trembling at the knees*
> *Just get there happily*
> *Doing what you please.*
>
> (George Formby)

"Who...?" I hear you say – if you're young!

Chapter 9

Two Policemen and a Norman Wisdom song!

What's this all about... I hear you say? Well, two very true funny stories to follow...

As a constable in her majesty's constabulary... (the Police for you younger ones) I was travelling along the seafront with a rather large colleague – known as junior. We were in full Police uniform, in a marked police car, when I reminded him of a rather silly little song I had sung to him earlier. It was by Norman Wisdom and the delightful Joyce Grenfell, in which they sing a little ditty, where Joyce begins a *la di da...* and Norman joins in out of tune etc., and then goes into roars of laughter, losing his breath etc...

When I repeated this, Junior began to laugh... and as I did so he laughed more and more, and then cry-laughed more and more... and he was still driving the police car along a crowded road... Can you imagine the other motorist's reactions when they looked guiltily at us, only to find two Policeman convulsed with crying laughter...[1]

Don't blame me!

The other story also very true:

> One of my late aunties had a big, sloppy lummox of a dog called "Fred". Anyway, she got up one morning to discover my uncle's false teeth missing... After a short search she happened to glance around at the dog to see him with a beaming grin on his face... "Oh look!" she said. "Fred's smiling at us! How nice..." only to discover he was somehow wearing my uncle's teeth in his mouth causing this surprising brilliant "steradent" white grin!

So if you are laughing... then so much the better

My point in this chapter is... *it is the simple things in life that make us laugh and smile.* Not the violent aggressive world we live in and see, day to day. If you can go out and find some simple laughter, not *at* others but nice stuff! Then your health will improve ten-fold.

Ken Dodd – and his happiness song – says it all: Laughter is the best medicine, even Jethro (although a bit naughty) does the same thing in making us laugh

So what ever your poison in making yourself laugh, get out there and find it. Make the world a happier place, and *enjoy* it in the making.

---

[1] *The song that got to Junior was "Narcissus", by Joyce Grenfell and Norman Wisdom.*

Chapter 10

Accept. Accept. Accept.

This is written for therapists, just like me, who have the most irritating habit of trying to change everyone they meet. So, for once in your life...

STOP!   STOP!   STOP!

At this point we must do what we tell our clients to do... turn ourselves inside out. Sit down once a week, on your own, and look inside your own head to see what is going on in your brain.

To do this, try some simple relaxation techniques... e.g. Sitting quietly, with your eyes closed, visualising your thoughts. What sort of images do you see? Pictures in colour or in black & white; does this show you anything you need to change about yourself? You may see people's faces, or events in your life, which you or need to change

Sometimes, trying to change someone *before* they are ready to change, can be a bad thing, for it is the individual who needs to recognise that... change before the... *CHANGE* can take place.

Sometimes, just a nudge in the right direction is all that is needed for a brain to be reprogrammed

A gentle suggestion, reflection or showing the person another way of doing things, is an excellent start.

Acceptance of all things is the way to a happy non-judgmental free life. Take me, for instance, as a gay man myself, I am at this moment sitting in the high street of a very gay Sitges, in Spain. As I sit here I can see, passing by, different people of all shapes and sizes. For one moment I began to think that they are not my type of person at all... but *is that judgmental or what?*

Judgmental, judgmental, judgmental.

So. Here I am. The same, but different. Judging people as they go by. *My* internal workings are unique, and so are *theirs*... which is *their right,* as are mine!

So whatever you think of the person; their dress code; their skin colour; someone with one leg, or a disfigured face...

STOP AND SAY

I accept difference and celebrate diversity...

Accept. Accept. Accept.

Exercise
Close your eyes and say silently to yourself... *seven times...*

> *I accept difference*
> *and celebrate diversity*
> *with unconditional love*

...and whilst you do this, picture in your mind *whatever it is that you have a hang up about* and CHANGE THE PICTURE *for something that you really love. e.g.* a person... or maybe a favourite pet... etc., so that you are retraining your brain for acceptance.

Remember
Most bullies are reformed bullied people. They thrive on your fear and rely on seeing you shrink into a corner, or run for cover.

When you turn around and confront them – remember that *YOU* have *THE RIGHT* to do this because *you* are the one who is *free*, not them! Watch them *RUN* for cover, and squeal!

If you are in a minority group yourself, a good place to start the acceptance feature is on *yourself*. This is due to the fact that very often it is US who has a chip on our shoulders?

> *Everyone is born and everyone will eventually die. So why not embrace our fellow human beings rather than play war games with the world?*

Chapter 11

Just get out there and live a little

I have just finished reading the book *The Secret,* by Rhonda Byrne – a book well worth reading, believe me, as since the day of starting to read that book, my roller-coaster of life has started big-time, at a fast rate of knots. This book basically explains that *we reap what we sow*, which is a very well known phrase indeed.

Michael Neill states the same in his book *You can have what you want*! Another truism, because *you* know, and *I* know a lot of you will straight away doubt! You really can achieve *anything* if you decide it's what you want. It's the moment you *doubt* it, or tell yourself what you *don't* want, that things go wrong.

Believe me when I say I am one of the worlds biggest doubters, it really *does* work when you order things from the universal law shop!

So, the big NLP'ism here is:

No doubt   No doubt   No doubt

Don't blame me!

Try this...
Close your eyes and picture something you *really* want to achieve. Then tell yourself you **WILL** *achieve* it (not when or how) just that you will. Then gauge from 1 to 10 how wonderful that feels

NOW, think of a thing you *don't* want, and feel how negative this makes you feel.

*SO WHICH TRAIN OF THOUGHT DO **YOU** PREFER?*

Practice this every day...

> But *ONLY* on things you *DO* want.
> *NOT* on the things you *DON'T* want.

Your life will take off just like mine did and you wont look back ever again...

GO TRY!

Getting out there, living the life, includes taking risks; some calculated, and others just going for it, because *you know* that *you never know* what's around the corner. – Here today gone tomorrow! – So don't bother looking, because if you keep looking around corners, you may just come across, dare I say it, *A DEAD END!*

> *You* can do
> whatever *you* want to do in life,
> starting NOW!

Just get out there and live a little

Oh dear... I can hear that eternal motor bike... *But But But But But But But But...*

FOR GOODNESS SAKE.
You only get ONE life
(each cycle that is).
SO GET OUT THERE
*AND **LIVE** IT!*

Remember

- It is *YOU* that *makes* the journey, no one else
- *YOU choose* the journey, no one else!
- *YOU choose* the restrictions that *YOU* put on life, no one else.
- *YOU choose* the bends and dead ends, no one else.

So YOU, and only YOU, can choose to *CHOOSE TO CHANGE THE ROUTE.*

Then throw the tom-tom away and go on the journey *of discovery and recovery...NOW!*

Footnote

I spent twenty-five years in a very controlling organization called the Police *Force* – not *service* as it is now called – which was full of misguided, bullying managers and *politically correct* bosses – or managers as they now call themselves.

Don't blame me!

It was only when I decided to turn this around and move on into early retirement that I turned this whole thing around.

Don't get me wrong, there were, and still are, some very good people in the Police, but they are restricted by *politics*. But hey! This turned my life around so that I could live in a very sunny happy place like Spain, and since that date I have never looked back

SO THINK ON THIS!

If *I* can do it, so can *YOU*.
The choice really *IS* yours?

I moved to Spain with no job and very little money – but a lot of guts and determination – which made me walk into a totally alien set-up and get a job and fly… (speaking no Spanish at all!).

It has taken me about five years of hard self-work to let go of a restrictive lifestyle *But I DID IT,* and so can *YOU*, and a lot quicker if you read lots of life books and do the exercises etc.

Chapter 12

Designer labels

It doesn't matter what designer labels you wear, it's the *way* that you wear them that matters. I hate designer labels, as such, except when the quality of them makes them worth the money.

It doesn't matter *what* label we wear it's *why* we wear it that hurts.

I used to wear a uniform at work, and when I first put it on I used to love it. But at training school *ye olde woman sergeant*, with a broad brummie accent, said *"you will, some day, want to get home and out of that uniform as soon as you can"* and boy was she right.

Take a look around you at the people in formal clothes. Sometimes we think *"look at those posh people"* or *"look at those snobs"*. But strip the uniform off (so to speak), and guess what? We are all the same underneath.

People with a uniform fetish just love it. But most

who wear it to work just cant wait to get out of it! *WHY?*

When I put my uniform on I felt invincible, fearless strong etc. etc. But *without* it I realised it was a front!

It *does* command respect, and in that context it works – to an extent. But as a community officer I was respected *because of how I worked* (not always, or indeed very rarely, by the book). Others who wore the same uniform were hated.

> This proves that it is the *INNER* person
> that is the important factor,
> *NOT* the external looks

Getting back to designer labels, why do you think people wear them? Is it because they think it makes them into something?

In reality, most people who have worked for their money dress very plainly, as they don't want to stand out in a crowd.

So, are labels a bad thing do you think? Do wearers "*people please*" when they wear them?

Experiment
Sit in a public place and count the labels on passers by, and as you do it try to guess what they do

If you're brave enough, ask them afterwards, and I bet you will be surprised at some of the answers.

Designer labels

Try this
I did this; I sat under a tree on the seafront, looking across at a posh hotel, and its clients, imagining what it would be like to be there.

I imagined it so much that I then walked across, to the terrace and sat down, a very la-di-da place indeed, I ordered a sandwich and a glass of wine, and a coffee. *GUESS WHAT?* I didn't even look at the price! Well done me!

FOR THAT MOMENT I became a label that everyone looks at!

The *big difference* was that I would be just as happy at Joes café, with a bacon sarnie. WOULD *YOU*? (Joe must be very rich by now he is so famous with his label.)

So what's the point, you may ask??

Well, we all label people at some stage in our life, be it regarding colour, race, sexuality, rich, poor, whatever...

Another name for this is...

JUDGEMENTAL

so

CUT IT OUT!

Practising *acceptance,* of all things, on a daily / hourly basis, will make you *feel SO good* – honest!

Chapter 13

Bloody 'ell, it works!

One of the many things that Paul McKenna, Michael Neill, and Richard Bandler taught me was how to...

> *ELIMINATE SELF-DOUBT,*
> ***PERMANENTLY***
>
> *How do you do that?*

What you do is just sit and relax, close your eyes – as many times a day you get chance to do – and...

> *CONGRATULATE YOURSELF*
> for *anything*, however big or small,
> *YOU DO RIGHT IN THAT DAY.*
>
> *I DID THAT WELL*
> *I DID THAT RIGHT*
> *I DID IT – I DID IT – I DID IT*

Now, pay attention
When I write in BIG LETTERS or **bold print**, *OR IN BIG ITALICS*, close your eyes and...

Don't blame me!

REPEAT, REPEAT, REPEAT,

...as this reinforces the thought and boosts your brain chemicals to change from the *negative* to the *positive*. This will make you feel, and be, much better!

You can say things silently or out loud, (don't be shy now) – *The LOUDER the better*

And as you do it say in a big loud voice–

SWWWISHHHHHHHHHHHH...
SWISH SHSHSHSHSHSH...

...for a few seconds, just after the words.

A free shot of adrenalin without the needle!

When you do *anything* in my book, or indeed *anything anywhere*.

SMILE SMILE
LAUGH LAUGH SMILE

As it's the *best medicine* for *any* hang-ups. Ken DODD was right – good old ham!

Chapter 14

Meditate to mediate

Quite often I ask clients "h*ow often do you meditate?*"

More often than not, of course, the answer comes back as "*Oh I just don't have the time!*"

    WELL. WHAT UTTER RUBBISH!

You mean to tell me that doing this hard and often painful journey of ours, as we do, you don't deserve just ten minutes a day out of your day... for *ME time*.

    Just 10 minutes?

    *WELL YES YOU **DO** HAVE TIME*
    it's your *right...*

Go to a place, any place you feel comfortable with, turn off the phone...

    *I said **OFF**,*
    not SILENT OR VIBRATE...

...***NO*** doorbell, no nagging partner or mother in law (he he):

Sit down and slowly switch off...

When you first start doing this, your whole life slows down a pace or two, or more, and you will find that you deal with conflict, in whatever guise, in a more relaxed but positive, non-aggressive way.

You approach life with a different map to the territory you are involved in and *WOW* does it change your outlook on life.

Suddenly you can see the angle from the other person's point of view, which enables you to mediate the situation well.

Remember
You can start off SOFT
on any situation and get harder...

BUT

It's *impossible* to start AGGRESSIVELY
and then get softer...

Exercise
Take two chairs and sit on one, thinking of a time you got angry with a situation or a person.

Picture that in your mind: Is it in colour or black & white? Still or a moving picture?

Then swap chairs and think of a time you were really happy and calm: Add lots of colour, building the picture stronger with each breath. Build it up *stronger* and **stronger**.

Then
Swap chairs back to the angry one again and *force* and *squash* the angry picture out, *ELIMINATING IT TOTALLY AND FOREVER, replacing it with the good picture... And...*

SWWWWWWIIIISSSSHHHHHHH!

Open your eyes and shake your head a few times to break the thought. Now, try to think of the angry scene again?

WHERE'S IT GONE?

Meditation can be addictive, but in a good way. Try to... *no, DO IT* every day of your life and you will enjoy all things, even the so-called bad things wont be so bad!

P.S.
You don't need posh stools or cushions or music to meditate, just be comfortable and quiet and use some music you like to do it with.

Eventually you will progress to the best type of meditation to...

STILL THE MIND...

SILENCE!!!!!!!!

Don't blame me!

It's the most powerful of all, when you can achieve it... to allow your brain to be totally silent!

Remember

Say to yourself... This is *MY* life and I have the *RIGHT* to do this and I have the *RIGHT* to *quality of life*.

Chapter 15

The grand finale

Well I do come from a theatre background you know (Stephen Holroyd aunty Pauline and all).

No, seriously... to end this short first attempt at a book, we can go through our lives *LIVING IN THERAPY*, as many people do. I once met a person who had done over *twenty* anger therapy workshops. I think that would make me angry rather than cure it!

OR

We can perhaps seek the psychiatrists chair for a brief time, so to speak, and then take the risk and the challenge of life and...

...get out there *and*
LIVE!

We will make "*mistakes*", although in my mind they are usually just lessons;

Don't blame me!

We will *see, hear and feel* challenges in our lives; move on and become better people from the experience;

We will *do* things which we later regret: Well, don't dwell on them. Just go *onwards and upwards!*

We will come across people and things that we *do not much like*. Just let them pass by, *with love and light*, or surround them with flowers in your mind and they will disintegrate in front of you;

We will often feel lonely and down: Well *Get out of that rut*, challenge it and enjoy the bumpy ride ahead.

I did, and still do, and look what happened to me!

God Bless you and with love and light I wish you the success I am finding on my Journey.

Remember.
We are all unique individuals who deserve respect, happiness and love. It's all out there for you to discover...

GO GET IT!
NOW!

The author

Peter Blyth is a cognitive therapist, qualified counsellor and an internationally licenced NLP practitioner. Following 25 yrs as a community policeman, on some of Britain's most challenging estates, the author was trained in NLP by some of the best life coaches in the world, including; *Paul McKenna, Michael Neill* (The Hollywood life-coach) and *Dr Richard Bandler* (inventor of NLP in America).

He now lives in north east of Thailand. Isaan. With his partner.

E mail: *peterblythspain22@yahoo.co.uk*

Useful Websites

* Paul McKenna's Training
  http://www.paulmckenna.com/
* Paul Mckenna's Books etc.
  http://www.mckenna-direct.com/cgi-bin/at.cgi?a=313271
* Information about Paul Mckenna
  http://en.wikipedia.org/wiki/Paul_McKenna
* Richard Bandler - official website
  http://www.richardbandler.com/
* Information about Richard Wayne Bandler
  http://en.wikipedia.org/wiki/Richard_Bandler
* John Grinder - official website
  http://www.johngrinder.com/
* Information about John Grinder
  http://en.wikipedia.org/wiki/John_Grinder
* Michael Neill's Genius Catalyst site
  http://www.geniuscatalyst.com/
* Wiki on NLP
  http://en.wikipedia.org/wiki/Neuro-linguistic_programming
* NLP information
  http://www.nlpinfo.com/
* List of NLP topics
  http://en.wikipedia.org/wiki/List_of_NLP_topics
* History of NLP
  http://en.wikipedia.org/wiki/History_of_neuro-linguistic_programming

CPSIA information can be obtained
at www.ICGtesting.com
Printed in the USA
LVHW091609141020
668800LV00026B/421